8/07

LABRADORS

by Susan H. Gray

The Child's World®

Published in the United States of America by The Child's World®
PO Box 326 • Chanhassen, MN 55317-0326
800-599-READ • www.childsworld.com

PHOTO CREDITS

© Ariel Skelley/Corbis: 27
© Corbis: 9
© iStockphoto.com/Erik Lam: cover, 1
© Jean Louis Aubert/PhotoAlto/Alamy: 19
© Jim Craigmyle/Corbis: 25
© Josh Reynolds/Associated Press: 23
© Juniors Bildarchiv/Alamy: 17, 21
© Mark Raycroft/Minden Pictures: 13, 29
© Studio Paggy/IZA Stock/Alamy: 15
© Renee Morris/Alamy: 11

ACKNOWLEDGMENTS

The Child's World®: Mary Berendes, Publishing Director;
Katherine Stevenson, Editor

Content adviser: Mary Feazell, Secretary, Labrador Retriever Club, Inc.

The Design Lab: Kathleen Petelinsek, Design and Page Production

LIBRARY OF CONGRESS CATALOGING-IN-PUBLICATION DATA

Gray, Susan Heinrichs.
  Labradors / by Susan H. Gray.
    p. cm. — (Domestic dogs)
  Includes bibliographical references and index.
  ISBN 1-59296-775-2 (library bound : alk. paper)
  1. Labrador retriever—Juvenile literature. I. Title. II. Series.
  SF429.L3G73 2007
  636.752'7—dc22   2006022638

Table of Contents

NAME That DOG!

What is the number one dog in America? ❀ What dog is loved by almost everyone? ❀ What dog swims well? ❀ Did you guess the Labrador (LA-bruh-dor) retriever (ree-TREE-vur)? ❀ You are right!

5

The Wrong Name

Labrador retrievers did not come from Labrador. They came from Newfoundland (NOO-fund-lund). Labrador and Newfoundland are both in Canada. Labrador is on the east coast of Canada. Newfoundland is an island right next to it.

In the 1800s, a traveler in Newfoundland saw "small water dogs." They were called Saint John's water dogs. They were named for St. John's, a city in Newfoundland.

The map on the left shows where Newfoundland is on Earth. The map on the right shows a closer view.

Greenland

Iceland

Baffin Bay

Hudson Bay

Labrador Sea

Labrador

Ontario

Quebec

Newfoundland

C a n a d a

New Brunswick

Nova Scotia

U.S.A.

Atlantic Ocean

7

Hunters used these dogs to **retrieve** birds they had shot. The dogs often retrieved birds from the water.

People who fished probably took the first water dogs to England. One Englishman decided he wanted some water dogs for himself. So he had some more brought to England.

Years later, English people still had Saint John's water dogs. But they no longer used that name. They called them Labrador dogs. That name was wrong, but it stuck anyway. In 1903, this **breed** was named the Labrador Retriever. People call the dogs Labradors, or Labs, for short.

Over time, Labs were taken to other countries. Some came to America. Today, they are America's most **popular** breed.

Labradors are said to have worked with people who fished. The dogs would leap into the water to retrieve fishing nets.

This Lab looks almost as if he's smiling! You can tell he loves playing in the water.

A Big, Smart Dog

Labradors are large dogs. They are about 21 to 25 inches (53 to 64 centimeters) tall at the shoulder. Adults weigh about 55 to 80 pounds (25 to 36 kilograms). That is about as much as a fifth grader.

Labs have two coats. They have a soft, thick under-coat. This fur keeps them warm. They have an outer coat of short, straight hair. The outer coat feels hard to the touch.

This Lab is watching a squirrel run across the yard.

11

A famous writer named James Michener once wrote about the Lab. He wrote that the dog looked so smart it might speak. He added that it "seemed always about to smile."

Water rolls right off the outer coat. After a swim, a Labrador dries quickly.

Labs can be black, brown, or yellow. The brown color is called "chocolate." "Yellow" Labs can be reddish, golden, or almost white.

Labs have dark brown eyes. Their noses are black or brown. Their ears hang down. Many people say Labradors have kind faces. Some say the dogs look smart.

Labs' tails are thick at the base. They are covered with heavy, thick fur. Some people call them "otter tails." Otter are furry, swimming animals. Their tails have thick fur, too.

Here you can see the three different Lab colors. Which one do you like best?

13

The Dog That Has Everything

It is not surprising that Labs are number one! They have everything people want in a dog. They make great family pets. They are gentle and friendly. They are careful with children. They even let kids use them as pillows! They get along well with other pets. They do not growl at visitors. And they love to please their owners.

Labradors are also smart and easy to train. Owners teach them all sorts of tricks. The dogs learn tricks quickly.

This Lab has been trained to balance a ball on its nose.

15

Some Labs learn to do high-fives. Others ring a bell when they want to go out.

Labs love to be busy. They like to hike or jog with their owners. They also love to swim. They swim out to retrieve tennis balls and sticks. They are ready to do anything their owners want.

Some Labs play a game called *flyball*. A flyball box has a hole in one side. It has a pedal on the same side. The dog runs up and steps on the pedal. A ball shoots out of the hole. The dog runs and jumps to catch the ball. Some dogs play this game for hours.

American President William Clinton had a Labrador. The dog was a chocolate Lab named Buddy.

Catching a ball can be tricky! This yellow Lab does it easily.

Little Labs

Labrador mothers usually have about eight puppies in a **litter**. Some have only four or five pups. Others have as many as 14.

Newborn Labs weigh about as much as an orange. Over their first few months, they grow quickly. Labs grow faster than many other dogs.

Labrador puppies are helpless at first. They cannot walk. Their eyes do not open. They cannot hear. They cannot chew food. They drink only their mother's milk.

This Lab mother is resting as her puppies drink her milk.

The puppies' first few weeks are important. The pups get stronger and start to move around. They become able to see and hear. They start to play with each other. Some of their playing looks like fighting! But they are learning something important. They are learning how to get along with other dogs.

The puppies also learn how to be around people. They keep getting bigger and stronger. Soon they are ready to be with people all the time. They are ready to be part of someone's family.

All dogs gain weight quickly at first. In their first year, Labs gain more than 50 pounds. This is more than 100 times their weight as babies!

This older Lab puppy is playing with a ring toy.

Labradors on the Job

Labradors make great pets. And many people use them as hunting dogs. They are good at other jobs, too! They have a great sense of smell. This helps them do police work. They can sniff out drugs or stolen goods. They can also track down missing people.

Labradors also help **rescue** people who are lost or in trouble. Labs have found people buried in deep snow. They have found people under buildings that have fallen down. The dogs pick up the people's **scent**. Labs have helped save many lives.

This Lab is learning how to find people trapped by earthquakes or storms.

When a service dog is working, people should leave it alone. They should not pet it or bother it. The dog needs to pay attention to what it is doing.

Some Labs work as **service** dogs. They help people inside and outside of their homes. **Guide** dogs help people who cannot see well. They walk with their owners to the store or to work. They help them cross streets and stay safe.

Other service dogs help people who cannot move around easily. These dogs do all sorts of things. They turn lights on and off. They close doors. They retrieve things the people drop. They bring the phone. They open the refrigerator. They even pull wheelchairs!

This Lab is guiding its owner through a shopping mall.

25

Caring for a Labrador

Labradors are full of energy. They need to exercise and run around outside. It is not good for them to stay indoors all the time.

Even though Labs do not have long fur, they still need **grooming**. They need to be brushed. Sometimes they need a bath.

Bathing a Lab can be messy! These kids are giving their Lab a bath outside.

Most Labs are healthy. A few have problems with their eyes. They get **cataracts**. Cataracts are whitish spots on the eye. Dogs cannot see clearly through cataracts. Animal doctors, called **veterinarians**, can remove cataracts.

Labs' main health problem is with their hips. Sometimes Labs' leg bones do not fit into their hips well. This can be painful for the dog. It can even keep the dog from walking. If the problem gets bad, a veterinarian can help.

Many Labs go through life with no big problems. They often live to be 10 to 12 years old. Some live even longer. And they are lots of fun to have around!

Labs are always ready to have fun! This Lab is resting near a lake before playing some more.

29

Glossary

breed (BREED) A breed is a certain type of an animal. Labrador retrievers and golden retrievers are different dog breeds.

cataracts (KAT-uh-rakts) Cataracts are whitish spots on a person's or animal's eye. Cataracts make seeing difficult.

grooming (GROOM-ing) Grooming an animal is cleaning and brushing it. Labs need to be groomed.

guide (GIDE) To guide people is to lead them or help them find their way. Guide dogs help people who cannot see well.

litter (LIH-tur) A litter is a group of babies born to one animal. Labrador litters often have about eight pups.

popular (PAH-pyuh-lur) When something is popular, it is liked by lots of people. Labs are popular dogs.

rescue (RESS-kyoo) To rescue something is to save it from danger. Some Labradors help rescue people.

retrieve (rih-TREEV) To retrieve something is to find it and bring it back. Labradors are great at retrieving things.

scent (SENT) A scent is a smell. Labs are very good at finding things by scent.

service (SUR-vuss) Service is work that helps someone. Some Labs work as service dogs.

veterinarians (vet-rih-NAIR-ee-unz) Veterinarians are doctors who take care of animals. Veterinarians are often called "vets" for short.

To Find Out More

Books to Read

Jones, Robert F. *Jake: A Labrador Puppy at Work and Play.* New York: Farrar, Straus, & Giroux, 1992.

Macaulay, Kelley, and Bobbie Kalman. *Labrador Retrievers.* New York: Crabtree Publishing, 2006.

Stone, Lynn M. *Labrador Retrievers.* Vero Beach, FL: Rourke Publishing, 2003.

Wiles-Fone, Heather. *All About Your Labrador Retriever.* Hauppauge, NY: Barron's Educational Series, 1999.

Places to Contact

American Kennel Club (AKC)
Headquarters
260 Madison Ave, New York, NY 10016
Telephone: 212-696-8200

On the Web

Visit our Web site for lots of links about Labradors:

http://www.childsworld.com/links

Note to Parents, Teachers, and Librarians: We routinely check our Web links to make sure they're safe, active sites—so encourage your readers to check them out!

Index

About the Author

Susan H. Gray has a Master's degree in zoology. She has written more than 70 science and reference books for children. She loves to garden and play the piano. Susan lives in Cabot, Arkansas, with her husband Michael and many pets.